I0152748

Hiccups Haunt Wilson Avenue

Hiccups Haunt Wilson Avenue

Poems by

Marilyn Zelke Windau

Kelsay Books

© 2018 Marilyn Zelke Windau. All rights reserved. This material may not be reproduced in any form, published, reprinted, recorded, performed, broadcast, rewritten or redistributed without the explicit permission of Marilyn Zelke Windau. All such actions are strictly prohibited by law.

ISBN: 978-1-947465-67-1

Kelsay Books
Aldrich Press
www.kelsaybooks.com

*Dedicated to my grandchildren
with a fond appreciation for childhood*

Acknowledgements

I would like to thank the following for their publication of these individual poems:

Ariel Anthology: "Apron"
Brawler Lit: "A Childhood Visit"
Kind of a Hurricane Press: "Birthday Pie"
Silver Birch Press: "A Box," "Long Overdue," "Under the Arch of Elms"
Verse Wisconsin: "Piano Fingers"
Your Daily Poem: "The Perfect Tree"

Contents

About the Author

Made-Up Stories

Walking home from school,
staring at cement sidewalk squares,
there are stories to be concocted—
stories to be made up
to tell at supper,
at bedtime—
stories you say are true,
stories you swear by,
by and by,
stories, which,
when told often enough,
become truth,
like Wonder Bread,
like Bactine,
like boasts to the bully
down the block—
shock and awe stories
so that you can live
to enter 3rd grade,
to use so that
you don't have to
clean your room,
take out the garbage,
walk the dog,
babysit your brother,
memorize the verse for Sunday.
You can pocket the stories
for later use, for children
who don't want sleep,
for grandchildren who do,
for journals insightful,
for generations,
stored in attics,
ready, always ready,
for discovery.

City Morning

Elm trees cathedral arch Wilson Avenue,
provide soft wind murmurs,
light green fluttering shade
in wet heat, late spring.
The smell of flagstone, border neighbors,
firecracker salvia, and drive-by exhaust
alert nostrils to city home.
Radio-alarmed wives at 6:15 on weekdays
wave men to the curb
to clear windshield seeds
and smog smudge
before oatmeal, coffee,
and lunch pail send them off.
Children roll over upstairs,
clinging sheet to chin,
dreaming it's Saturday
and neither school nor God needs them.
Mothers stare out the back porch window
furtively planning tomato crops,
perhaps sweet peppers,
before cocoa-coercing kids downstairs.

Home Place

We always came in the back door.
Dad would pull the grey blue Studebaker
down the Chicago alley
which paralleled Wilson Avenue
and into the garage.
Kicking open the stuck gate, he'd scrutinize
each of his tomato plants for flowers,
like a drill sergeant eyeing troops.

We kids would lug our school books
down the gangway in between the Johnston's,
never the Berlinghof's, house
to climb the three stairs to the back door.

Sometimes my brother would lurk
in the dark of the basement's outside stairs
and "Boo!" my sister and me.
We'd shout in fear and then in outrage
to "MOM!"

The kitchen held butter cookies,
which we fastened to our fingers
and ate scalloped, petal by petal,
slugging down slurps of fat milk.

It was the front entryway
where I would find silence and solitude.
Only the mailman noised that area.
"Clank!" declared the storm door's droplid
as four cent stamped envelopes fell to the floor.
"Clunk," voiced the lid on a trapped Life magazine.

There in the linoleumed entry was a bookcase,
old and oak with lift up, push back,
bevel glassed covers.
On the third from the top shelf, I'd pull out
a small chestnut leather volume,
plunk myself down on the floor, open it,
and pretend.

Ballerinas in tutus, long, short, bejeweled,
and in toe-shoes with crisscross-laced leg ribbons,
danced its pages.
In pliés or tour jetés,
in first position or in arabesque,
I whirled on air current dreams
to my future as Clara or Giselle.

Home in childhood was as black-white
as those pictures:
Yes, no, time to get up, time for bed,
set the table, put your toys away.
Ice box cake for dessert!
Sometimes dreams really can come true.
I curtsy-danced with mine in a book.

Gulley Washers

When it rains gulley washers in the city,
kids toe-heel off their shoes,
peel, ankle down,
their soaked, elastic-held sox,
take a quick look at the front window,
and spying no mom, run to the curb.
There, ready with leaves, twigs, ants, worms,
they ship out yard-nature to the rain rivers.
Their hair pitter-patters water to shoulders,
creating horseshoe, wet shapes on shirts.
Crouched at the cliff of the street,
they drop their veined vessels
with insect cruisers to the tumult.
Leaves, stem-tillered, draw shallow eddies,
zoom from 5010 to 5012 to 5014,
down the block.
At the corner, the round-the-corner kid
waves the winner in.
Intent on the races,
ears distracted by pelting,
children don't hear maternal shouting.
The oldest sends the signal.
All retreat from street,
reconnoiter at downspout,
removed for brainwapping.
No hairwash required tonight,
Mom's happy now, too.

A Raining Memory

Was it Wren or Oriole?
No, it was Lark—the favorite cabin
at Forest Beach Family Camp,
New Buffalo, Michigan.
The bath water warm side,
not the polio cold water side, of the lake.
A week of sand dune slide mountains,
lanyards, ferns pressed
into plate-shallow plaster,
enameled copper with melted glass globs
for paint on palette-shaped pins,
slide-out Cokes from the red, lift top cooler,
exhausted campers to bunk beds.
"Top! I get the top tonight!"
Closer to the open-beamed ceiling
of warm-weather wood,
I cozied into cotton covers
waking at once to plinkplink,
plink on roof planks,
a running rhythm of rain,
a percussion of safety soothing to slumber.

Four Square

In the city, everything is square.
Dormer windows and porch milk boxes,
coal chutes and skate keys,
sidewalks to school, sidewalks to home,
sidewalks to the store for square boxes
of Wheat Chex, Triscuits, Velveeta cheese,
buildings of scratch-your-bare-shoulder brick,
sliver-your-skinny-arm clapboard,
scruff-up-your-elbow stucco,
all are angled off to be right.
But to be square in the city
is to play times four,
with chalk, out in the street,
having a lookout for cars,
a lookout for older kids,
an ear out for fire sirens,
supper shouts,
ice cream truck bell yodels.
The owner of the small rubber ball
sets the time, the place,
the rules of the day.
Winner takes ball,
becomes bounce king of the block,
at least until tomorrow,
when we square off one more time.

Hopscotch

City sidewalk cement squares
called to every kid on the block,
and round the block, too.
After school, before supper, and later,
until dusk light failed
and streetlights bore first glow,
play was on.

Hopscotch was the event.
Throw the pebble.
Hop over one, land a foot in two,
two in threefour, five, sixseven,
eight, nineten,
Skyblue!

I had long arms.
I could throw to ten, no sweat.
I had long feet, too.
Touch a line, lose your turn.
I lost many a turn
until I became a toe dancer.
Then, with shortened, vertically-fraught feet,
I tossed and padded my way.
from nineten, with an airtwirl to Skyblue!

Once reached, the return trip was easy.
The joys of heaven, known, challenged anew.
Counted competition for the night was testy.
Recount was regular.

The streetlight, now mature in its illumination,
signaled adults to call us home.
Winners were back-pounded,
runners-up nah-nahed.
Heaven would wait
for tomorrow's faithful.

Good Humor

When the day's heat is beyond human temperature,
fathers, who barber the summer lawn,
are not in good humor.
They stoop-bow to regain a hula-hoop, a ball,
a troll doll, a left skate.

The down-the-block man
in the rectangular boat-paper hat,
with the bicycle bell chi-chinging,
and the icy treasure box on wheels,
he's Good Humor.

Kids' ears are music-pulled to the corner
and back, their order memorized.
Crunch, coated, cold—
summer relief has its price.
Relief can be a pitcher for adults,
but for kids, it's ice cream.

"Please, Dad? Please?"

Sticky to the stick,
tongues with splinters
are summer wounds,
gratefully gained.
Sweet torment.

Dad's Nose Noise

The almighty,
blow the door open,
gust the fire out,
send the kite up
to the stratosphere
SNEEZE.

Then the foghorn,
football game megaphone,
thirty pound ham hock pig nose
SNORT
into an eight inch square
white cotton handkerchief
stuffed quietly,
holding all that power,
into a deep pants pocket.

A Box

Sometimes, when he came in the back door,
after arranging the car into the one car garage,
maneuvering it in from the alley
at a 90-degree angle,
having dodged other cars, newer cars,
up thousands of numbered blocks in the city,
from downtown to Jefferson Park,
he still smiled.

Giving her a kiss on her left cheek
and a cross-arm hug to us three
at his knees,
he produced from under his topcoat,
the herringbone one
with the two inch grey buttons,
a box.

One inch thin, five inches wide,
ten inches long, white,
with gold cursive lettering,
it said, "Fannie May Candies."
We, the three, whooped with joy.

The box was set on the kitchen counter.
At dinner, we ate every vegetable we saw.
We licked our plates with tongues,
with fingers, readying for the joy.

Ceremonially, the box was presented
first to mother, who claimed
an "M" for a maple cream.
My brother, who was youngest,

was offered it next.
He looked for the calligraphy of "C"
and bit into chocolate chocolate.
My older sister finger-touched
row one and two and then with urging
selected "H" to match her name initial,
bit into hazelnut and smiled.

My turn was difficult,
because I knew what I wanted.
I wanted "V" for vanilla buttercream,
Dad's favorite.

I looked, stretched my finger,
changed direction and chose "R"
for raspberry.
It was scrumptious.

Once, Dad guided my hand back,
gave me his "V."
I gave him a brown drool grin
to return the love.

The Five Second Rule

Food which has dropped to the ground is safe to eat
if it is consumed within five seconds after falling.

When I was seven years old,
Mom accidentally sent a piece of mush-melon
flying off her knife
to the red brick-patterned linoleum kitchen floor.
I had a total of five seconds to stoop,
grab, and pop.

My mouth didn't know the rule.
It waited, and not for long.
I was a quick study,
with longer arms than my brother or sister.
I understood that five second rule.

It helped that I was skinny, like my dad.
I needed the nourishment,
that sweetness of orange melon,
soft to the teeth,
creamy to the tongue.

Mom shouted at me,
even though she was half Scottish,
and didn't like to waste anything.

Dad took the other half of the melon,
scooped vanilla ice cream into it,
adorned it with garden raspberries,
carried it to the living room, savored it
while listening to WTMJ radio.
His Milwaukee Braves were thus far
winning in the 7th inning against the Cubs
and Hank Aaron was up to bat.

25

The Perfect Tree

I am in the corner of the front room
at 5010 W. Wilson Ave., Chicago, Illinois.
My phone number is Pensacola 6-8616.
I am 6 years old and watching my dad
create this year's perfect Christmas tree.

Fat, glass, football-shaped, colored lights
8" apart, strapped to each other by braided wires
wait quietly in a musty cardboard box at my feet.
Two prongs at the black rubber socket end
jab my bare ankle above white doggy slippers.

My chenille bathrobe is warm and too short.
It used to be Helen's,
but I'm even taller than she is now.

Dad has in his hand a drill
with a funny looking, U-shaped crank.
He is lying on the carpet,
his balding head under pine branches,
his glasses tilted, eyes squinting
at the task:
to fill in boughs where boughs are needed.

A pen knife whittles spare branch ends
and with a shove and a twist:
"Ah, that's better!
How does it look, Snooks?"

"It's beautiful, Dad!
Can we put the pretties on now?"

Apron

My father wore an apron
while making vegetable soup.
He wasn't ashamed
to wear women's garb.
He loved soup.
He'd watched as a boy
as carrots, potatoes, parsnips,
cabbage, onions, celery,
and peas drowned in broth.
Resuscitation was necessary
with parsley, pepper, garlic,
and salt.
It was the tomatoes that shouted
for an apron's pants' protection.
Red as blood, splashed tomato stains
required cold water soak and time.
His brow would simmer
at the apron stain.
Then he'd sniff,
lift his mother's wood spoon to lip,
sip and nod,
savoring tomorrow's supper,
knowing the pants could ride
the train downtown
and return.

Fascination

On the elm lined streets of Chicago's north side,
sunlight filters, speckling sidewalks.
Around the block, friends call—
ring their bike bells insistently.
A skinny worm crosses the puzzle
of light pattern in front of me.
I sit down and watch,
slowing Saturday to a crawl.

Aunt Nell

We lived in a bungalow,
not a Sears' diagram, put-it-together house,
but a clone house, just the same.
It was in Jefferson Park,
bricked, in Chicago, on the northwest side.

There were gangways,
narrow passageways,
between the houses,
to establish personal parameters
for neighbors' comfort.

Still, with next door's second floor windows
open to our view,
we snickered at Aunt Nell in her nighty.
We, two sisters in our lavender bedroom,
her color choice, snuck peeks,
and giggled quietly, so as not to disturb
the blue-haired, pin-curled woman before slumber.

We'd laugh, sharing a double bed
with a single bed size quilt,
until sleep caught us unawares.

I'd wake, shivering,
tugging to no avail,
thinking how warm
repose could be
alone, upstairs
next door,
like Aunt Nell in her solitude.

Across the Gangway

Dorothy Johnston lived next door to us.
Her house looked, from the outside,
absolutely the same as ours,
red brick bungalow, five steps up
to the front door landing,
a gangway in between.

She had two sons, Stevie and David,
the same age as my sister and me.
My brother didn't count to them.
He was younger, no threat.

Her husband's name was Morton,
like the salt.
Every time we'd go downtown Chicago
on Edens Expressway, we'd see the huge sign.
I'd always ask, "Is that sign
about our neighbor, Dad?
"When it rains, it pours." "Morton Salt."

"No," he'd say. Just no.
I never did think so,
because it was a little girl on the sign,
blonde, blue dress, holding an umbrella,
tipping the cardboard canister of salt.
If it had been about him, it certainly
would have been a boy doing the pouring.

They had this ugly blue car that they parked,
as everyone did, at the curb on Wilson Avenue.
The car looked like a stuffed chicken,
with big haunchy thighs.

It was never there during the day.
He drove it to work. She didn't, but did—
work, as a wife and a mother,
though I didn't realize it then.
We had a Studebaker. It was blue, too,
but not robin's egg, stand out blue.
It was cool springtime sky blue.

She was like Beaver Cleaver's mom.
Dorothy wore pearls, housekeeping her throat.
She wore dresses, not "housedresses."
Her husband's aunt lived with them,
mostly in the room with the dressing table,
shining those little lights at night,
so she didn't see the creeping crepe skin.
We saw her. We spied.
She spied, too.

If the floor plans of the houses on our block
were the same, it meant Aunt Nell had to go upstairs
from the kitchen, pass through Stevie and David's
shared room, listen to their guffaws nightly
to get to her sanctuary.

It meant that winding her blue-grey locks
into pin curls was meditative,
and wrapping the quartered scarf around them,
tying it centered to her forehead
was closure to yet another day.

Young girls across the gangway peering
were no insult.

She saw their invasion of her privacy
as a learning experience for them.
She hoped they would stand strong
against her nephews.
She admonished Morton, her brother,
frequently, to bring them up right.

Telling Tales

The Chicago Public Library strongholds
a bazillion books.
My mother carried most of them
in twist-paper-handled, brown bags
to and from the Jefferson Park Branch.
Each week Helen, Butchie, and I
would walk two on her left,
one on her right, holding hands,
a coat pocket, or sleeve cuff.
Sometimes, we'd just touch pinkies.

The journey of four city blocks brought tears.
We'd have to let go of Sal and her blueberries.
We'd have to say goodbye to Glinda and Toto.
The pictures, page turned for a week,
were relinquished to a lady behind a counter
we weren't tall enough to see.

Excitement replaced melancholy
when we came to the stairway climb.
We hung on banisters of oak
like jungle monkeys grasping overhead vines.
The second floor children's room brought the hunt:
the pulling, the pawing, the clasping to chest
of each big, thin, sturdy discovery.
A circus at sunrise, holes dug to China,
trouble with Dick or Jane, new friends next door,
star names and word games,
colors and capital letters.

Two feet of literature checked into Mom's bag
for the quicker trip home.

We couldn't wait.
Helen went upstairs.
Butchie went under the kitchen table.
I found the bathtub with my blankie and book.
We memorized illustrations until bed,
when it was Mom and Dad's telling tales time.

By then, our ears could see
what our eyes had learned.
We listened to the story we knew,
again and again.
We turned it over in our sleep, nightly,
until the next week's library surrender.

I'm Telling

Used to be that when you said,
"I'm telling," it meant a story
was coming soon.
It meant it was your turn,
or your dad's at bedtime,
or your mom's on the way to church,
in the car with your white,
almost spotless gloves on.

I remember those words differently.
"I'm telling." meant that I was in big trouble.
My sister had seen me do something horrible,
or my brother had had it with girls,
two girls as sisters, and couldn't take it anymore.

"I'm telling." meant one of them
was snitching to mom or dad,
Grandma or Great Aunt or
whoever would listen and
dispense justice.

I'm not innocent of voicing these charges.
I used these words a lot, daily,
many times daily.

I remember being heard
by the supreme court of children.
I remember that witnesses
were called, interrogated.
I remember that cases
were solved, justice imparted,
punishments imposed.

Sometimes I went to bed smiling in rightness.
Sometimes I went to bed crying and penitent,
but plotting to win my case tomorrow.

Childhood Indiscretions

Those of you who are second children,
especially if your sibling is of the same gender,
you know!
You know that you have to try harder,
be more daring, perhaps dangerously bolder,
to be noticed.

My sister, two and a half years older,
was my watchdog.
"You have to do what I say! Mom said!"

I never thought
that she might take the blame
for my indiscretions—
and indiscretions there were.

She played with her Ginny doll
while I pulled mother's first edition books
from the front hall bookshelf,
and proceeded to rip pages out of them
just to hear the sound.

She was in the bathtub with me
when I decided the water was too warm,
jumped out, ran down the hall,
out the front door,
and down Wilson Avenue to Lawler.

Being of young age, our bath time was early,
about seven o'clock.
I can't hear them now, but I'm sure
all the neighbors laughed and shouted—
in Danish and German, in Yiddish,
and Polish.

My mother in blushed English,
apologized, gathered me in a towel,
later chastised my sister for letting me get away.

This incident was long after I fell out
the front porch window.
No one saw me, so no one knew
if I'd landed on my head or my bottom.
It wasn't a severe drop, only about three feet.
There were flagstones though,
bordering the flower bed.

My sister continues to believe it was my head
for how else could I have turned out to be such a nut!
She didn't recognize my creativity.

That spring I snuck down the block
to pick every neighbor's tulips.
All the houses were brick.
They all had front steps.
They all had a gangway in between,
an alley in the back by the garage.

I believed all those tulips were my garden,
ready for harvest: reds and yellows and purples.
Mom put them in vases,
apportioned them back to the neighbors,
gave my sister a talking to.

I am repentant now,
sorry for the pain I caused my sister.
I was little. What did I know?
In high school, she made me wear "Villager" skirts,
the "in" clothes.
I felt that was enough pay back.
We are even.

Nut Cups

From my fourth birthday party on,
I knew what to look for.
It was not the paper tablecloth my mom bought,
its folds showing the 8" x 12" packaging limits.
Once she got Sleeping Beauty,
once Cinderella.

Once it was Lady and the Tramp
and I blamed my older sister.
She loved it. I didn't.
I preferred the Legend of Sleepy Hollow.
"You can't have that. It's too scary," she said.
"You're not the boss of me,
and it's MY birthday!" I proclaimed.
A November birthday is close enough to scary,
close enough to Halloween.

What to look for was not the plates mom bought.
They were just plates, paper plates.
Then there was the plastic silverware—
a new invention which impressed the neighbor moms.
Kids didn't care. We wanted sweets.

It was the nut cups!
What meant it was really my birthday were the nut cups!
Their discovery was enough
to send my childhood heart into arrhythmias.

Nut cups meant it was really true.
Friends were coming.
They were bringing smiles
and presents.

I would wear a crown.
I would sit at the head of the paper table cloth.
Games would be played.
Laughter would sound in the house.
I would go to bed happy, full
of sugar and mirth,
and the peanuts, gumdrops,
and love of my family,
all presented symbolically
in a pleated paper cup
overflowing with joy.

Hollyhock Dolls

I was in the alley behind my house on Wilson Ave., Jefferson Park, Chicago. I left the front yard's shadow-filtered light of arched elm trees when my older sister, Helen, went to play with her friends.

"You're too little," she said.

My younger brother, Ray, said he was with Roy and Dale and that they were after bad guys at some gulch.

I raced through the gangway between the red brick, almost arms-out touchable bungalows, stopping short at the back yard. I could hear Arthur Godfrey on the radio laughing with my mom on the back porch. They were ironing out some laundry problem together.

I snuck by the garage, past Dad's tomato plants, and out the back gate to the alley.

There they were, in all their midsummer glory of color—hollyhocks! Some had flowers of tissue paper red and pink on their sturdy stems, which reached from my waist to above my head. I pushed aside the plate-like leaves to pluck three beautiful blossoms: doll dresses!

Cicadas blasted my ears, bicycle bells rang out, and somewhere down Avondale, Al's ice cream truck stopped its tune for a sale.

The garage shadows grayed the gravel beneath my feet.

The neighbor's dog pressed his pink heart nose through the fence slats, intent on knowing my game.

Under puff cloud blue skies, I was playing dolls, hollyhock dolls. They danced and laughed and felt like summer in my hands.

"A" Words

I think I knew the word "aggravate."
I think I'd heard my mother or father use it.
I think I even knew what it meant,
when it involved me, my sister, or brother.

I didn't know the word "aggregate."
I learned that one many years later.
Its meaning though was very real to me.
It was that pebbly, granular, gravelly feel—
smooth, yet rough—
of the drinking fountains at Wilson Park.

There were three of them at the entrance.
Circular, and on pedestals that flared out
at the bottom—like phosphate glasses—
I was just a little taller than they were.

Around and around them I would walk,
with my left hand following their texture.
I could see that on the inside they were concave
with a multi-holed drain at the center.
They reminded me of kolaches,
those little pastries my mom would buy
at the Czechoslovakian bakery up on Lawrence.

Circle puffs of baked golden dough,
a lake of apricot or raspberry
or ick! prune filled the center.

Water filled the middle of the fountains.
It burbled quietly from one inch metal tubes,
four to each fountain.

They didn't make a spray or an arc.
They just bubble-spilled over the tubes
onto the aggregate.

Sometimes, if mom wasn't looking,
I'd put my thumb over a tube.
Sometimes I could reach two tubes!
The water really rose high then in the others,
and, if my sister was trying to get a drink,
she sure got one—right in the eye!

I think that was one of the times I heard
that other "a" word: aggravate.

Kindergarten: Mayfair School

Red brick, majestic, with white-sculpted trim,
it could have been the Houses of Parliament,
the Hermitage, the cathedral in Siena
I'd seen in books.
Its three stories tall seemed skyscraper-high
to a kindergartener.

We lined up at the bell, the warning bell,
the "you'd better stand up straight,
have all your belongings: your homework,
your lunch, your milk money" bell.

Two separate lines, one for the girls,
one for the boys.
No budging, no hitting,
no "Na-na-a-booing."
We marched in with mittens pinch-clasped
to our coat sleeves, our galoshes thumping
their furry tops to our calves,
thumping soles to the foot-curved concrete steps.

Up and in, coats and accompaniments
to our lockers, hair finger-straightened
as best we could, boys laughing at efforts.

The big room for kindergarten!
Alphabet letters bordered the blackboard:
upper and lower case letters,
just in case Mrs. Newman asked.

She asked for numbers as well.
Up there at the base of the blackboard,

more at our height, they were seemingly
more important: 1 through 10.
I liked the letters better.

Bathroom mats were cushy pads for naptime.
Before that, milk and cookies:
glass pint bottles with cardboard circles,
sealing in the cold white.
Pull tab released, big gulps satisfied.
Cookies from home:
sometimes Old Dutch windmills,
mostly Salerno butter cookies,
my favorite.
A hole in the center, scalloped edges,
they looked like flowers to be eaten
a petal at a time, as the finger revolved.

After naptime, we built fantasy structures
with shoeboxes, covered to look like bricks.
Then out for recess, where we chased
and ran away from boys, or from anyone
designated that day to have "cooties."

Once I was the designated "cooty."
I learned not to play that game anymore.

There was a "park" on the school grounds:
lilac trees in the springtime,
with their lavender perfume.
We nosed them, picked individual petal cones,
stowed them in pockets, snuck our hands in
to treasure their perfume all afternoon.

Under those trees, we sat with classmates,
told secrets, grasped hands,
pledged that we were best girlfriends forever.

My sister and brother and I walked home together
from Mayfair School to 5010 W. Wilson Avenue,
to our house and our yard and our toys
to await the next adventure,
the next school day at Mayfair.

Clothes Shopping

It was either Anne's Department Store
or it was Reznik's
or Wolke and Kottler's.
Mom continued to make the mistake
of taking all three of us kids
clothes shopping together.

I think this time it was because
my sister and I needed new gloves for Easter.
We were required to wear
short white gloves to church.
We also would wear them to play
dress-up, and to dig in the sandbox.
Consequently, we went through numerous pairs
of these pious hand-hiders annually.

My brother needed new white shirts.
One Sunday morning my dad had to find
a discount store to buy him one
because only discount stores were open
on Sundays.
It seemed that all my brother's other white shirts
were either dirty or ragged.
We were generally late to church.

While at Anne's Department Store,
I discovered that clothing was hung
on circular racks.
It didn't take me long to find a way
to the inside of this clothing column.
I simply parted the hangers of dangling dresses
on a rack near the boys' shirts.
Once in the middle, I could hide, hoping they'd seek.

And seek, they did, but to no avail.
I wasn't going to give myself away.
Mom called the store manager for help.
He was gruff when he found me.
Apparently, this was not a new game to him.

Embarrassed, my mother led us all out the door.
On the Montrose Avenue sidewalk,
I got a good/bad talking to.

She went back later, after Dad got home,
to buy two pairs of white gloves and
a boy's size 4 white shirt.

God forgave me, but I'm not sure my mother did.

Odd Eggs

In the alley behind our house
strange sounds would emanate
on a regular basis.
At least once every two weeks
we would hear a loud, shrill,
screechy noise.
Sometimes it woke us kids up.

Mom, being downstairs in the kitchen,
recognized this sound.
She told us, as we were coming for breakfast,
that she would be right back.
Of course, we followed her to the back.

The strange noises came from a cart,
pushed by a tiny man.
He was dressed all in black, in a suit and a tie.
He had curly sideburns and a beard.
He wore a black hat.

Mom said he was the scissors grinder.
He came down the alley seeking work.
He sharpened scissors and knives.
This was just one of his jobs.
He also shouted, "Odd Eggs!" repeatedly.

I asked my mom, "What does that mean?
What are odd eggs?"
She said, "He came here from another country.
He can't speak our English very well.
He uses the sounds of his language.
He's saying, "Old rags.""

He wants our old rags.
He wants anything that we don't want anymore."

"Would he want my doll, Mom?
The one whose leg broke off?
Would he want my sweater—
the one that's too small now?"

"I'll ask, Snooks.
You stay there.
Don't open the alley gate."

Mighty Mouse

I loved Mighty Mouse.
He flew into my life
on Saturday mornings
to save the day.
He had big ears
to buoy him on air currents.
His chest was broad and muscular.
He was brought to me by Wheaties,
the breakfast of champions.
On TV, he defended weak maiden mice.
I was a maiden, thought mouse-weak.
Dad said, "You can do anything
you set your mind to."
I wanted a Mighty Mouse muscle shirt
to prove I could.
I didn't get the shirt but I got the attitude.
I relinquished weakness,
gained the flight power,
learned the boy stuff,
did the deeds.
I still eat Wheaties.

Air Raid Drill at Mayfair School

It didn't seem scary—
when we heard the siren.
It wasn't like the fire drill screech,
that high pitched, soprano scream.
It was more like an "OOOOOH"
voluming upward in strength and surety.

We were scooted by our teacher
out into the hallway,
told to "Duck and cover!"

This was an air raid drill.
We were in 2nd grade:
Mrs. Summerhill's class.
We put our coats or sweaters
over our heads and backs
as we crouched on the floor,
our knees in our mouths.

A chubby boy in my class wasn't able
to get down that low without it hurting.
He cried in pain, stifling his lack
of toughness in his shirt cuff.

We couldn't stay in our classroom
because the windows were twelve feet tall.
Two panes, one up, one down.
They were raised and lowered by a seven foot pole,
wooden, strong, allowing a city breeze to enter,
if a breeze there was to be had.

The atom bomb, in its brilliance of light,
would have blinded us through those windows.
"Don't look at the light!"

We had to "Duck and cover."
The Civil Defense squad told us so.
My dad had a pamphlet:
"How to Survive the Atom Bomb:
Build a Shelter."

We didn't realize then, but this was serious.
We were just kids, learning to follow directions.
This was not just a reprieve
from a spelling test
or arithmetic time at the blackboard.

No napping in the hallway was allowed.
No snickering, no chit-chat.
We were prepared,
on the third floor of Mayfair School.
We were ready.

Our government told us
the Russians had an atomic bomb.
They could at any moment deploy it.
Our only chance at survival
was to "Duck and cover!"

I listened. I wasn't fat.
I could bend, to a point.
I had a good teacher.
I survived.

I went down to our basement storeroom many times
to find amongst the canned goods, the cookies
stored in what Dad thought was a safe place,
our fallout shelter.

Shadows and Hide

When I was little, I escaped the world.
 I went into the gangway,
that corridor between city houses
which offered shadows and hide.

Beyond calling distance,
of mother, of sister, of brother,
I had my own time—and
spaces for fairy tales, for stories,
for moon escapes, for play.

There was no one to please,
no one to admonish,
no one to encourage
or discourage my imagination.

I play, now!
No one has to know.
I don't have to hide
these thoughts, these places
my mind makes up.

I don't have to tell before I go to bed.
I don't have to ask for forgiveness.
God is not going to mind.
I don't have to agree to wear the plaid skirt
picked out for me for tomorrow.

I can go to school and learn.
I can put my coat over my head in the hallway.
I can wait for the bomb to drop.
I don't know death.

I know Mom and Dad, my sister and brother.
I know tomorrow is a school day,
with outdoor recess and friends.
I can imagine naptime and dream again.

Walk

My dad used to say
we all needed to walk a mile
in another man's moccasins.
I had moccasins.
They were hand-me-downs.
They were Minnetonkas.
They were smooth earth ochre,
comfortable,
with soft fleecy linings.
I had never walked a mile before.
I walked until I cried,
and then sat down on the trail.
I could have been picked off
by the proverbial bobcat,
who strikes the weakest link.
There were no lurking predators
that day in the north woods.
Dad picked me up and carried me
the last feet of the journey.
It's hard to walk a mile
in another man's moccasins.
My dad walked them first for me.

Cracks

As we walked to school,
my sister would shout at me every time!
"Step on a crack, break your mother's back.
Don't you like Mom?"
I did. I loved my mom
but I was fascinated by the sidewalk lines.
I didn't know then their cause:
the pressure of freeze/thaw,
the pressure of ages of feet pounding,
rasping the concrete.
To me, at that time, the lines were rivers,
valleys of miniscule civilizations
whose inhabitants were just out of sight.
They hid in the dandelions, the plantains,
in the creeping Jenny and Charlie
bordering the pavement.
On Saturdays, I looked for the citizens,
the people of the cracks.
I found a plastic cowboy leg once
and a fabric petal from a tiny dress.

Snuffy Dog Food

One time, when I was six,
Mom and I went to Dell Farm,
the grocery store on Lawrence Avenue.
We needed to buy groceries and dog food.
Dad usually goes.
He has dogs' eyes begging in his brain.
He even remembers his dog, Rover,
from when he was five.

I brought along my new purse.
It was an Easter present:
white plastic, with an enveloped front fold
that featured artificial flowers.
I remember they were pink.

I was so proud!
It was an adult possession.
It meant that I had valuables.

When mom and I went off to find
cans of Snuffy dog food,
I left my new purse in the cart.

Gone! It was gone when we returned!
No money had been in it.
Why would someone want it?
I learned a lesson that day.
Things of value need to be kept close.
I still remember that purse, and that lesson.

On Account of Savings

First there were gifts of pennies,
with Lincoln's head on them.
He had a big nose like my dad did.
Pennies would buy chewy red candy coins
at the drugstore by Wilson Park.

Then, as my teeth fell out, I was presented
in the dark of night with quarters.
I found them under my pillow.
My sister told me there's a fairy
who collects teeth! Go figure.
I knew a boy who collected stamps,
another who saved bugs,
and my friend Lois had dolls lined up
on her bedroom windowsill,
all with different bride dresses on.

Sometimes I saved the quarters in a little bank.
It was shaped like a baby pig—
not much space for not much money.

I started getting an allowance when I was ten.
My sister, brother, and I were requested,
or, rather, required to do chores.
"Fair is fair", my parents said.
"We're a family. We all have to work together."

I knew I was a grown up
when my dad took me to Hoyne Savings Bank.
Together, we opened a bank account for me.
Now instead of real money,
I had numbers in a folded paper book.

I was counted as an adult,
on account of my account.

I miss the pennies, warm in my hands.

Fishing Green Lake

We walked down to Uncle Marlyn's pier
early in the morning. It hadn't rained.
"Rain stirs up the bottom. All the food rises,
like ice cream in a chocolate float.
The fish don't bite.
Would you, after being at the soda fountain
at Woolworths?" Dad asked.
I was as skinny as the pole I held,
patiently, for dad to do my worm.
I was a girl. Girls don't do worms.
Dad knew that. He was kind.
My brother made a face.

I snap-whizzed my lucky line,
bobber and all, to the green of the lake.
Steady eye. Steady eye.
Ever vigilant.
I was well trained in the art of fish possession,
having caught two blue gills
and a perch in my illustrious history.
A small wiggle, just the tiniest of movement noted,
and I jerked that pole as if someone
had attempted abduction of my teddy bear.

"Reel him in! Reel him in!" my father shouted.
I was cranking as fast as my fingers would rotate.
"Rest! Let him rest for a little."
"How about me?" I said, "I'm tired, too."
Dad was there with the net,
as I brought the biggest fish I'd ever seen
to the surface.
It must have been 14 inches long.
I could see that it was longer than a school ruler.

"It's a northern," Dad said.
"A northern," I told my brain.
"A northern," I boasted with pride.
"Too little," he said. "Have to throw him back."
I cried.
My brother made a face.
How could my dad, my kind dad,
take the fish's side over mine?
"It's the rule," he said, "I alone don't make the rules.
All of us who want fish forever make the rules."
Appeased, I snap-whizzed my line again.

Black Cherry Rice Salad

I was a kid.
I was seven.
We were at Uncle Marlyn's
in Green Lake, Wisconsin.
I was used to Wilson Avenue
in Jefferson Park
in Chicago.

I loved cherries.
Whenever mom bought a jar,
two hours later she would
ask me to stick out my tongue.
The jar had gone missing.
My tongue betrayed me.
I was red with guilt.

So when my aunt said,
"Black cherry rice salad"
all I heard was cherry!

We sat to eat in their basement.
They called it the lower level.
It had the same picture windows
as the regular floor
but no carpets, just linoleum squares
holding us to hopscotch
while waiting for lunch.

We weren't allowed to play
 the one-armed bandits—
"What's a one-armed bandit, Dad?"
that Marlyn nickeled his brother
out of every time we visited.

We saw the lemons click fall
in a row,
but those cherries!
When's lunch?

Dad always said my eyes were bigger
than my stomach.
That day, he was right.
Maraschino? Black?
What's the difference?
I gobbled and knew I'd been betrayed.
What cherries were these,
trapped in moosh rice and celery?

My stomach voiced disapproval
as I ran upstairs
to the bathroom.

Visits are cut short
by short beings—
children who don't know
their own stomach minds.

I look for stems still
on bright reds
atop ice cream,
avoid fruit salad upsets:
cherry bombs.

Medicine

The door opened.
A needle-sharp point of light stabbed me awake.
"Lick the spoon," Mother said, "Swallow."
I was hoping for bubblegum—
flavored pink,
even lemon,
or blackberry,
but it was a tablespoon-awful,
not a teaspoon-sootheful.
My head was a cloud of fuzz blanket.
Her words whirred my ears.
I licked the spoon, swallowed
to recover
sleep.

Edens Highway Ruined My Life

I was eight but at 6's and 7's.
I didn't want to change.
I didn't want to go.
Why did they have to put in that big road
down by the pumping station?
Why couldn't I still go to Mayfair School?
St. John's?

ST. JOHN'S?

I closed the door of the cedar closet behind me.
Boy, there were a lot of clothes in there.
I sat on the floor,
pulled mom's long dark green formal—
the one with rhinestones around the satin cuffs—
across my crossed legs
hiding this fraidy-cat
body and rebel-stubborn mind.
I hummed in my throat.
I peeked at all dad's pants, his top coat,
the shelf of hats, mom's purses.
They'd never find me here.
My ears were intent on foot sounds.

I fell asleep.
It was dark in the closet.
It became dark outside in the hall.
I was missing. They were frantic.
When mom said police, I quietly emerged.
I still had to go to St. John's.
I learned to play chess and I memorized eight hymns.

Piano Fingers

"She has piano fingers—
long, skinny—
like the black keys.
She should take lessons.
Both of the girls should."
So, after that,
it was off to Mr. Placko
every Wednesday.

I sat.
Helen played,
learned to read music,
progressed to head nods.

I liked the rests the best,
played by ear,
by memory,
by golly.

Mr. Placko, the ruler of the Steinway,
had a stern way with 12" of flatwood.
The stinging of knuckles supposedly sent nerve
responses to synapses which
controlled rote notes.

I hated Mr. Placko.
I liked his gingko tree though.
It was outside,
protected by borders
of city sidewalk.

A Childhood Visit

The Scotty dog, our only toy,
knew how to behave.
He, who stood stiff-legged,
closed-jawed,
black, in the corner,
under the window seat,
with perked ears,
listened.
He knew.
He had a red plaid collar.
He was stuffed, not allowed at table.

We were,
but not to speak.
Great Aunt Anna, with tight, gray
braid-pinned, circle hair,
who Mom, through family rights,
called Annie,
served us ham, and dill pickles
from a barrel
in the back yard
in Milwaukee.
We saw it.
It was wooden and had scum
on the brine surface
where the pickles bobbed.

I didn't say a word.
I just threw up.
German was spoken.
The bathroom was tiled in black
and white. The towel was stiff

on my lip.
Courteous apologies were offered.
Come agains were proffered.

Dad drove home—
Mom's usual choice.
A White Sox game voiced
balls, not strikes.
I slept in the back window shelf
of the Studebaker,
all the way to Chicago,
purged.

Women of the Flame

We used to gather
on the back porch on Wilson Avenue
just before bed on summer evenings.
Our tired, melancholy mother
would seat my sister and I
at the card table, light a candle.
The floor was uneven.
The table would tilt-knock.
The cicadas frazzle-hummed
melodies of night.

"I see my sister Evie," she would say,
staring at the flame.
"I see Elsie at the farm.
I see my mother making bread.
The linen kneading cloth is bleached
white. She has smiling, floured hands."

Bobby pins poked my neck
and my chenille robe's fuzzy bumps
polka-dotted concave circles on my backside.

I saw Rapunzel, Glinda.
I saw my first dog, Corky.
I saw Mrs. Michael, my fourth grade teacher,
in pants, a suit coat, and galoshes.
Laughter was not allowed.
This was serious.
This was concentration.
This was seeking unity with those no longer with us.

We were women of the flame.
We saw there the past, memories of kin and kindness,
grasped at hope and remembrance
as easily as grasping summer stars,
or flickering candle fire.

Hope

"It's a skyscraper!" my brother said.
What did he know? He's a boy.
He didn't' believe in fairytales.
"Fairytales are for ger-rels," he would mock.

I knew! It wasn't a skyscraper.
It was Rapunzel's tower.
We both could see it clearly from our house.
It was just over there, far down Wilson Avenue.
It was a cylindrical, red brick tower.
So tall! We thought airplanes would hit it.

Why couldn't they rescue Rapunzel?
No prince was aboard!
No way to parachute down to save her.

We couldn't see her hair from that far away,
but I knew she had thrown her braid or
her brushed locks out the tower window every day—
ever hopeful, ever vigilant, ever ready to flee.

She had a cruel mother, absent.
I had a nice mother, absent sometimes.
I waited for her kiss and hug, nightly,
when she got home late from teaching.
Rapunzel, I knew, wasn't as lucky.

It's really a water pumping station
coal-fired exhaust tower.
I didn't know all that until several years ago.
I still think of it as a waiting place,
a habitat of ponder,

of what may come,
of what might happen.
The possibilities are endless.
The possibilities are hope.

Birthday Pie

It seems that I always got
pumpkin pie with candles.
My birthday being near
or on Thanksgiving
did not many years afford me
the floral sprays of pink roses,
lime green leaves,
and edge waves of buttercream—
only pumpkin pie
with the fork tined crust,
crust that I left uneaten on my plate.
Speckles of nutmeg,
cinnamon, and allspice
cook-floated and congealed
on the oil-shined circle of surface.
Candles helped a little,
but I longed for an annual
white creamy mustache
of frosting my brother and sister got.
One year, pecans were added
to my birthday pie.
The dog dragged it off the counter
where it cooled.
His gums turned upward in a grin.
I grinned, too.
He'd eaten the filling,
but left the crust on the floor.

My Best Gift: The Magic 8 Ball

It was a heavy 4" diameter black shiny sphere
with a cut off circle window.
I knew it was made for me.
It said so.
It was my birthday.
It said 8, my number.

The ball could roll.
Then it would totter and settle
onto its flat circle bottom.
But the ball wasn't meant to roll.
It was meant for magic.

Inside the circle was a dark oracle pool
into which surfaced words, directives,
answers to life's questions.
"Of course," it said.
"You may," it convinced.
"Not now," it cautioned.
"Try again," it urged.

When Dad and Mom were at work,
the ball became my mirror
of opportunity.
"Can I have this cookie before dinner?"
"Do I have to clean my room?"
"Can we get a puppy?"
"Can I trade in my sister for a room of my own?"

I always wondered about that circle.
Who had cut flat the sphere?
Who had exposed the mystery, the magic?
Why was I the chosen one
to receive its guidance?

It took me awhile, but I finally figured out
that my 8 ball had been sliced by Big Al
at his grocery and butcher shop
on the corner of Laverne and Avondale.

Now that I was eight, Mom allowed me
to walk the three blocks down to his store
to buy summer sausage for sandwiches.

I watched as Al's meat cutter machine
zipped off thin circles of lunch meat,
back and forth,
back and forth,
one circle at a time.

I thought of my magic ball.
I could just see the perfect black slabs
peeling off, floating to the floor,
the wafer thin messages unread,
the answers unrealized
by customers waiting
in the shoe-scuffed smooth wooden aisles.

Long Overdue

I'm reading Frank Dixon now.
It's a Hardy Boys Mystery.
I found it amongst your death's leavings.
The first page is mildewed.
It says, "After 30 days, return to Dave."

At bedtime, when I was eight,
I read Nancy's stories
of the moss covered mansion
and the broken locket
and the old clock, attic, stagecoach.
I was in love with Ned Nickerson.

You were curled up in your own room,
on the daybed, with your heroes.

Night pulled shades down at 9 o'clock
but parental rules mustered youthful ploys.
A flashlight beamed bright my sheet shelter.
In your room a night light was the factor at play.

Batteried lights didn't burn holes in blankets.
They only woke us kids at 3.
Then, after droop-eyed bathroom calls,
our legs shifted mystery dog-eared pages
to bed bottom,
where reading would be resumed,
tented,
tomorrow.

Pink

Sometimes we got to wear tutus.
They were pink.
They were made of tulle,
fabric with lots of holes in it.
It stuck out, fluffed out
of elasticized pink panty pull-ons.

We were ballerinas.
I was six. My sister was 8 ½.
We went for dance lessons
at Berning's Studio on Milwaukee Ave.
It was upstairs of an insurance office,
a long climb for a little kid.
I remember being tired on arrival.

It was a light-filled studio,
with narrow planked,
shiny smooth wood floors.
We faced walls that were mirrors,
floor to ten foot ceiling.
There were ballet barres, some high,
some low, for we who couldn't reach.

Zora, our teacher, was there, a stern presence.
She had red hair, wavy.
Her eyebrows looked like
someone had drawn them on her face.
She wore a black leotard and a flowing
"V" hemmed red skirt that was see-through.
Her lips were red as well.
She was strict with us,
let us know immediately

that no nonsense was allowed.
Stand up straight! Head high!
Look straight ahead! No smiling!
We were dancers, disciplined in our art.

My sister got to wear toe shoes,
pink shiny satin, with flattened ends.
She stuffed the empty toes
with angora fuzz, bunny fur,
then stuffed her feet into the narrow slots.
Ribbed on the soles with unbending slats,
her feet stayed in secure position.

Pale pink ribbons, about a foot
and a half long, dangled from the shoes.
She was taught, as I jealously looked on,
to crisscross those ribbons up her ankle
and calf, to tie them in a bow at the back.

I wore "flats," black, with an elastic band
at mid-foot. There was a lace to cinch
at the toe but it didn't cinch enough
for my skinny feet.

I never advanced to "en pointe"
as my sister did.
I did get to wear a tutu, though.
It was for a dance recital.
I was in the back row.
I hope it was because I was tall
for my age.
I was so thin that in the tutu
I looked like Saturn on a stick.

I can still do the first, second, third,
fourth and fifth position.
I can plié. I can tour jeté.
I can still see those beautiful pink
ribbons zigzagged on my sister's legs.

Gelatin Artist

Mrs. Krueger was renowned in our neighborhood.
Her gelatin salads were the talk of blocks.
My mother invited her to our house
when I was nine years old.
Eager to help, eager to learn,
I leaned on every word of instruction.

The jello mold was shaped like a Bundt pan,
looked like a castle with an interior moat
when inverted.
"The first layer we make will be the top,
so it must be the most splendid!" she said.
Raspberry gelatin with mandarin oranges
placed just so—alternated with maraschino cherries,
my favorite.
"Yes, you can have one...or two.
We must let it chill now."

The next layer was orange jello,
studded with pear crescents
and green grape punctuations.
The waiting, the chill time, was insufferable!

Then lemon jello with peach moons
and red grapes, confidently positioned.

Last, hours later, came the lime jello
into which we dropped
cantaloupe and honeydew melon balls,
round spheres of orange and green,
we had scooped from their shells.

Mrs. Krueger allowed me the leftover rind peaks,
the Alps of melon.
My mother smiled, knew she had a son, Floyd,
who was granted the same rewards.

The final touch at unmolding the castle of sweet
and fruit was to embellish the perfection.
I formed cream cheese into planets,
rolled them in crushed pecans,
others in chopped cherries, in toasted coconut.

A shredding of lettuce, the castle jiggling atop,
the planets circling in their orbit at its base—
it was a thing of beauty, too perfect to cut,
too spectacular to eat,
but eat we did.

Its deliciousness remains in my eyes, my mouth,
my memory of Mrs. Krueger,
an artist whose medium was gelatin.

Memory of a Queen

Little girls dream of princesses and queens.
They imagine jeweled crowns and scepters,
glass slippers, dances, thrones and princes,
coaches and footmen, velvet and satin,
red robes dragged up aisles,
easy waves and hand gestures meant to assure,
to quell questions, anxiety, needs,
to exhibit control, safety and kindness.

On July 9, 1959, I was nine and a half years old.
I lived on the northwest side of Chicago,
close to Lake Michigan,
a great lake on a chain of great lakes
whose waters flowed to the sea,
the Atlantic Ocean.
I knew there were queens across the sea.

My mother took us downtown that day.
We went to Navy Pier, a long concrete line
of mooring, a tie-up, an exhale in a voyage.
Ropes were thrown to hourglass-shaped
land-stays, circled and cleated to America.

We went then, grasping hands,
my mother, my brother, my sister, and me
to Soldier's Field, the arena of the Chicago Bears,
not for football, but for royalty.

We saw her from afar, Elizabeth at 33 years old,
a queen!

Her consort, Phillip, stood tall next to her, smiling.
They seemed to shine radiantly in the July sun.
I was in awe of their splendor.

In my jewelry box, now, at this age,
I protect the rhinestoned crown pin with flowing ribbons
that my mother bought me as a memory.
I remember it as a powerful day,
when a woman showed me strength and capability.
Sometimes that woman of memory is Elizabeth.
Sometimes she is my mother.

Fall of the House of Usher

It was a sunny afternoon in Chicago.
I was nearly ten years old.
I asked my brother to come with me
to watch a movie at the Gateway Theater,
which was about three blocks from our house
on Wilson Avenue in Jefferson Park.

He said no. So, being the second child,
I said, "I'm going on my own!"

That was my first, my lifetime, mistake.
I was tall for my age, but at ten years,
I barely could reach the ticket counter.
I gave my allowance money, was issued a paper stub,
entered the theater to find a seat in the dark.

The Gateway Theater aisles were narrow.
I found a seat easily because it was a matinee.
Not many people were in the audience.

The cartoons at the opening were fun.
I could laugh and relate to Scrooge Mc Duck.
The newsreel was another story.
Survival of the atomic bomb was featured.
President Eisenhower had given Chicagoans
fair warning that we were about to be bombed.
Dad had the Civil Defense brochure
on how to build a bomb shelter.
Newspapers related pseudo-Russian attacks,
noted where the non-bombs landed and
totaled how many Chicagoans had been killed
because they didn't leave work quickly enough,

didn't "Duck and Cover!"
The results of our "slaughter" were in the Sun Times.
I closed my eyes for most of the newsreel.

The feature film was "The Fall of the House of Usher,"
written by Edgar Allen Poe and starring Vincent Price.
It was intriguing at the start.

There came the time in the movie, however,
when there was a burial, of a woman,
her wooden casket being lowered into and covered with earth.

Then there was a scratching sound, repeatedly, from underground.
The woman had not died!
The lady was breathing the little air available and trying to get out.

Desperately seeking surface, her nail noise continued.
I shrunk down in my seat.
No one was sitting near me.
I couldn't call for comfort, for my mom.

It was dark out when I left the Gateway.
I hadn't figured on that.
I walked those few blocks toward home
listening to scratching sounds behind me.
I wrenched my neck turning to see
if the corpse was there trying to get me,
trying to live, trying to return
against all odds of family rejection.

I fled to my shared-with-my-sister room upstairs,
put on my footy pajamas,

got out my Nancy Drew book, my safe haven:
"The Secret of the Moss-Covered Mansion,"
pulled the covers up so that only my forehead bangs showed.

So many years later, I still cannot abide scary movies.
I see the vampire child at the window hovering
from "Children of the Corn,"
see the grotesque face of Chuckie, terrorizing my children,
hear scratching noises at the windows of our house,
though they are only birch tree limbs fingering my fear.

Hiccups Haunt Wilson Avenue

Outside, cicadas chirp-whine
and the D-shaped moon rises
devil phase over Dad's tomato plants,
the wooden clapboard one-car garage,
and the weed-cracked cement alley.

I am minutes away from teeth brushing,
from learning to spit quietly,
from passing Ivory over my face
with a Brillo-like, old washcloth.
Awaiting my turn at the sink
of the only bathroom for five,
I quietly porch screen-door out
to see the North Star.

They're always a surprise: hiccups.
These echo sounds
come on a body suddenly.
The occurrence is most usually
in a child, who hopes to be alone
at the time of affliction.
I fit the bill.

Thank goodness it wasn't daytime.
I wasn't with my friends Kim or Lois
or, heaven forbid, that stuck up
Suzanne.
I would have had to pay her off
in Juicy Fruit to not tell.

The hood of darkness hid my identity,
if not my noise.

"Hic! Hic! Hic!"
There was hardly time to take a breath
before the next throat barrage.

My brother, seeing his move,
grabbed my turn in the bathroom.
He wanted to read the next chapter
of his Hardy Boys mystery
before lights out.

I tried spinning.
I tried gulping and swallowing air.
I tried singing the ABC song.
I swallowed hose water for thirty seconds.
I didn't have a glass
for drinking water backwards.
That was probably the solution.

My chest ached with each new spasm.
I was sure they'd find my lifeless body
in the morning in the backyard,
my mouth open to exhale that last "hic."

Years have passed.
Wilson Avenue is quiet now.
Yet, I imagine my hiccups still haunt Wilson Avenue—
their sound reverberating
in the far reaches of the universe,
percussive sounds punctuating Pleiades,
giving push to shooting stars,
pummeling Perseus.

Dessert Days

Cookies for Halloween:
pumpkins with orange icing,
raisin features.
Green trees, jimmied at Arbor Day,
sugar-goitered turkeys for Thanksgiving,
silver drageed stars on Christmas.
No Lie Cherry Pie for Washington's.
Corn cob cast iron pan bread for Lincoln's.
A childhood of special treats
from an Illinois teacher mother
on her days off.

Neapolitan

When I was a kid
we got Neapolitan
ice cream in a box.
Flaps would be unsealed,
cardboard partitions pulled open.
A knife would be heated
under warm water,
slabs cut an inch thick.
It was a trifecta of color,
a cool flag on a plate.
My sister ate the pink stripe first,
my brother, the chocolate.
I cut across all the creamy bands,
put a narrow plank in my mouth,
was admonished for drooling
as puffed out cheeks
pulled my lips to a grin.

Under the Arch of Elms

The breeze would float elm leaves
like the little oval pancakes
we hoped for each Saturday morning
venturing out on a heat buttered griddle.

We'd lie on the grass in the front yard,
count as many as we knew numbers,
think of the serrated knife,
the bread knife,
try to slice pebbles
with elm leaves.

Summer heat trapped the upstairs
of a Chicago bungalow,
made us tired-cry
to sleep out under the arch
of elms.

We pedaled trikes, bikes
in their safe tunnel,
played hopscotch,
four-square, concentration
in the street
of their protection.

Summer green to fall yellow,
we blanketed our dollies
with elm warmth.
November gone, March emerged.
We followed their pattern
and grew, too.

I packed a suitcase
within their shadows,
moved my childhood to the suburbs,
heard they were ill.

Their dying did not open the sky.
Their dying did not open their limb-arms.
Their dying only offered emptiness, youth gone,
a grave under the arch of my elms.

Studio Couch

A brought-along, we might need it,
don't-throw-it-out item,
the studio couch became a favorite
curl-up, stretch-out,
pull-it-over, open-it,
spread-sheets-on-it,
necessary piece of comfort.

Mom would lie on the studio couch,
right wrist to forehead,
on the back screen porch
after lunch in the hot summer,
no wisp-of-a-breeze, afternoon.
WFMT tried cooling the airwaves
with Debussy's "La Mer."
The ice box hummed along
to Edison Electric's tune.

Chicago was always wet
with summer sweat
or winter bone-soak chill.

At Christmas, when relatives arrived,
my sister and I shared the studio couch.
Hauled in from the summer porch,
it was unfolded to its bi-level stature.
She, being older, retained the top level
and gloried, on Christmas morning,
in rolling down to wake me
from blanketed dreams of warm
Lake Michigan sand
and bug-juice ice pops.

Years later, I dragged it to the curb of suburbia
after its attic stay
for those many grown up years.

Three family dogs had learned
its softness on the sly.
Three children had raised its springs
in jumps of joy.
It was gone before the refuse truck
refused to take it,
collected, I hoped, by a thoughtful,
worthy, memory maker.

Tree Talk

Mostly, I need to sit and be quiet.
I need to clear my ears to hear those
which would impart wisdom of the earth.

I need to hear the catalpa tree
tell me about its big white flowers.
The catalpa is so proud of them,
but people don't value those flowers.
They wait for the beans!

Those long, sinewy brown pods
which hold the genetic formula
for another catalpa.
Neighborhoods wait for them
to decorate their Thanksgiving tables:
nature in abundance.

I need to hear the elm in our backyard,
a relative of the elms on Wilson Avenue
in Chicago, where I was born and raised.

Here, it has escaped the disease brought
from Holland, from the Dutch.
It grows tall, over my peonies, shades them.

I don't want either of them to lose the battle.
I'd seen that battle lost on my growing up street.

Mostly I need to sit and be quiet.
I need to listen to the trees,
to the flowers, the bushes,
the grasses, the wild, the natural.

I need to take in their language
of survival, of strength in change,
but mostly, of beauty, of spirit nurture,
of listen, and learn.

About the Author

Marilyn Zelke Windau, the middle child of three, grew up on Wilson Avenue in Chicago, where all the houses were bungalows made of brick and looked very much the same. Elm trees arched the street where she and her siblings played chalked games of hopscotch, four square, and concentration.

She remembers those youthful days of antics and lessons, and records them here, dedicating these poems to her newborn grandchildren.

At age thirteen she started writing poetry in high school study hall as well as in the dry bathtub of her family home with a pillow and a pencil. Her poems have been published in many print and online venues since 2007, when she was encouraged to get them out of a desk drawer to share.

Her chapbook *Adventures in Paradise* (Finishing Line Press) and full-length, self-illustrated manuscript *Momentary Ordinary* (Pebblebrook Press) were both published in 2014. *Owning Shadows* (Kelsay Books) was released in 2017.

Zelke Windau lives in Sheboygan Falls, Wisconsin—still very close to her beloved Lake Michigan. She is a retired public-school art teacher, the mother of three daughters, and the wife of an environmental engineer. She enjoys traveling, volunteering at the local art center for children's workshops, assisting in maintenance of public gardens, and helping to make poetry public through combined visual art and poetry exhibits.

She adds her maiden name when she writes to honor her father, who was also a writer.

www.ingramcontent.com/pod-product-compliance
Lightning Source LLC
Chambersburg PA
CBHW071105090426
42737CB00013B/2485